Tiger Sharks
Blue Blenders

DISAPPEARING ACTS

by Meish Goldish

Consultant: Nick Whitney
Postdoctoral Scientist, Center for Shark Research
Mote Marine Laboratory
Sarasota, Florida

BEARPORT
PUBLISHING

NEW YORK, NEW YORK

Credits

Cover, © Andrew Reid/Fotolia, and © stephan kerkhofs/Fotolia; TOC, © A Cotton Photo/Shutterstock; 4-5, © Design Pics/SuperStock; 6, © Purestock/Tom Brakefield/SuperStock; 7, © Seapics; 9, © Michele Westmorland/ Animals Animals Enterprises; 11, © Biosphoto/Soury Gérard/Peter Arnold Inc.; 12, © Jonathan Bird/Peter Arnold Inc.; 13, © Stephen Wong/marinethemes.com/; 14, © McKay/Levine/Animals Animals Enterprises; 15, © Franco Banfi/Photolibrary; 17, © Design Pics/SuperStock; 19, © ArteSub/Alamy; 20, © Sharon Morris/ Shutterstock; 21, © Jim Abernethy/Frink/gtphoto; 22L, © Pacific Stock/SuperStock; 22C, © Michael Patrick O'Neill/Alamy; 22R, © Juniors Bildarchiv/Alamy; 22BKG, © A Cotton Photo/Shutterstock; 23TL, © Design Pics/ SuperStock; 23TR, © Franco Banfi/Photolibrary; 23CL, © Franco Banfi/Photolibrary; 23CR, © maksimum/ Shutterstock; 23BL, © ArteSub/Alamy; 23BR, © A Cotton Photo/Shutterstock.

Publisher: Kenn Goin
Senior Editor: Lisa Wiseman
Creative Director: Spencer Brinker
Design: Kim Jones
Photo Researcher: Omni-Photo Communications, Inc.

Library of Congress Cataloging-in-Publication Data

Goldish, Meish.
  Tiger sharks : blue blenders / by Meish Goldish.
    p. cm. — (Disappearing acts)
  Includes bibliographical references and index.
  ISBN-13: 978-1-936087-43-3 (library binding)
  ISBN-10: 1-936087-43-X (library binding)
  1. Tiger shark—Juvenile literature. I. Title.
  QL638.95.C3G65 2010
  597.3'4—dc22

                    2009040123

For more information, write to Bearport Publishing Company, Inc., 101 Fifth Avenue, Suite 6R, New York, New York 10003. Printed in the United States of America in North Mankato, Minnesota.

112009
090309CGC

10 9 8 7 6 5 4 3 2 1

Contents

Watch Out! 4

Danger Above 6

Ocean Homes 8

Night Hunters 10

Using Their Senses 12

Deadly Teeth 14

Few Enemies 16

Baby Tiger Sharks 18

Helpful Stripes 20

More Disappearing Acts 22

Glossary 23

Index 24

Read More 24

Learn More Online 24

About the Author 24

Watch Out!

Millions of animals swim in the ocean searching for food.

All around them, the dark blue water moves quietly.

Below them, however, something is hiding.

It is a tiger shark, looking for its next meal.

Tiger sharks have dark blue or gray backs, which act as **camouflage**. This makes it hard for other animals to see the big fish swimming below them.

Danger Above

The tiger shark's dark-colored back is not the only thing that helps it hide in the ocean.

Most tiger sharks also have a white or light-yellow belly.

Animals swimming under a shark may not see the large fish when they look up.

The shark's belly blends in with the waters near the ocean's **surface**, which are brightened by the sun.

white belly

The average
male tiger shark is
about 12 feet (3.7 m)
long. Females can grow
up to about 15 feet
(4.6 m) long.

Ocean Homes

Tiger sharks live in warm ocean waters around the world.

Some tiger sharks have different homes during the year.

These sharks head north for the summer when the ocean waters in the south get too hot for them.

Then they swim back south for the winter when the northern waters turn too cold.

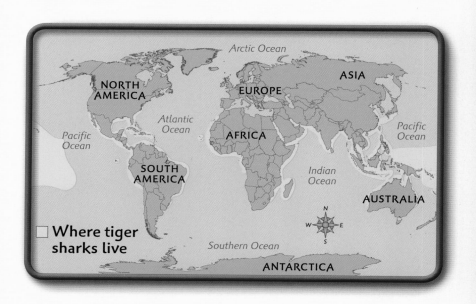

☐ Where tiger sharks live

tiger shark

Tiger sharks may swim up to 50 miles (80 km) a day. That's about as far as a car travels on a highway in one hour.

Night Hunters

When nighttime comes, the tiger shark is ready to hunt.

Without the sun, the ocean water is very dark, which makes it easy for the shark to stay hidden.

Other sea animals never see the big fish swimming near—until it's too late.

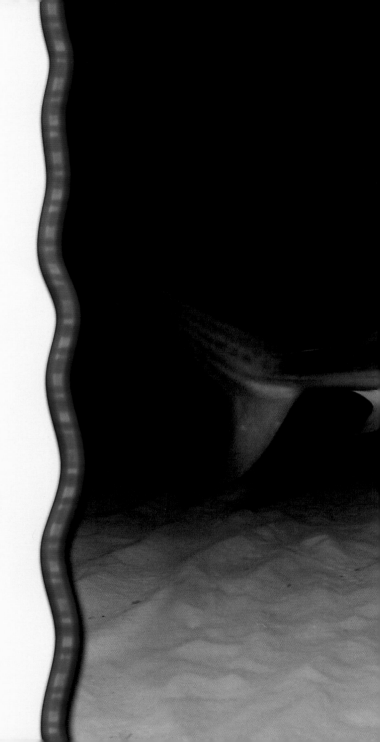
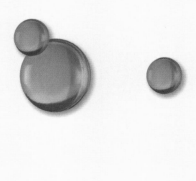

Tiger sharks usually hunt alone.

Using Their Senses

Tiger sharks don't always need to see the animals they are hunting.

Their good hearing and sense of smell help them find food in the dark water.

They can hear sounds made about a quarter of a mile (.4 km) away.

If **prey** is within 100 yards (91 m), these sharks can smell it.

A tiger shark's favorite foods include other fish, seals, dolphins, octopuses, sea snakes, birds called albatrosses—and other sharks!

Deadly Teeth

A tiger shark has razor-sharp teeth.

They can easily rip apart the body of almost any prey.

After a shark grabs an animal in its mouth, it is nearly impossible for the creature to escape.

The shark then either swallows the victim whole or uses its teeth as a saw to cut off pieces of the prey's body to eat.

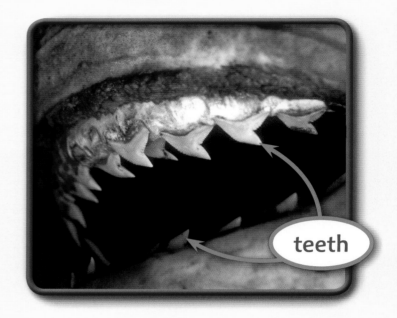

teeth

Tiger sharks will sometimes swallow trash that people throw into the ocean. They've been known to swallow glass bottles, leather boots—even steel oil drums. Tiger sharks are often called "swimming garbage cans."

Few Enemies

Camouflage helps some animals hide from danger as well as hunt for prey.

Yet tiger sharks have almost no enemies to hide from.

Few animals will go after a tiger shark if they see one.

The only creature brave enough to attack is a larger shark.

Tiger sharks usually swim slowly. However, they can swim fast if they're trying to escape danger.

Baby Tiger Sharks

In the late summer or fall, female tiger sharks have babies, called **pups**.

A mother may produce from 10 to 80 pups at one time.

Once they are born, she doesn't stay around to take care of her babies.

Luckily, the pups know how to swim and hunt all on their own!

Tiger sharks give birth to more babies at a time than almost any other type of shark.

pup

Helpful Stripes

A young tiger shark has dark **stripes** on its back, just like a tiger.

In fact, that's how the shark got its name.

The dark marks blend in with the ocean.

This is just another way that a tiger shark stays hidden in its watery world.

a tiger's stripes

stripes

The stripes on a young tiger shark start to fade as the shark grows older.

More Disappearing Acts

Tiger sharks aren't the only animals with colors that help them hide in the ocean. Here are three more sharks that are also blue blenders.

Great White Shark

Mako Shark

Blue Shark

Glossary

camouflage
(KAM-uh-flahzh) colors
and markings on an
animal's body that
help it blend in with its
surroundings

stripes (STRIPES)
the long, narrow
markings that
appear on an
animal's body

prey (PRAY)
an animal that is
hunted and eaten by
another animal

surface (SUR-fiss)
the outside layer of
something, such as
the top of an ocean
or river

pups (PUHPS)
baby tiger sharks

Index

backs 4, 6, 20

belly 6

blue shark 22

camouflage 4, 6, 16, 20

colors 4, 6–7, 22

enemies 16

food 4, 10, 12, 14, 16

great white shark 22

hearing 12

homes 8

hunting 10–11, 12, 16, 18

length 7

mako shark 22

pups 18–19, 20–21

smelling 12

stripes 20–21

teeth 14

Read More

Burnham, Brad. *The Tiger Shark*. New York: PowerKids Press (2001).

Murray, Julie. *Tiger Sharks*. Edina, MN: ABDO (2004).

Nuzzolo, Deborah. *Tiger Shark*. Mankato, MN: Capstone (2009).

Learn More Online

To learn more about tiger sharks, visit
www.bearportpublishing.com/DisappearingActs

About the Author

Meish Goldish has written more than 200 books for children. He likes to hide out in the various libraries near his home in Brooklyn, New York.